Read & Resp

FOR
KS2

Read & Respond

FOR KS2

Author: Celia Warren

Commissioning Editor: Rachel Mackinnon

Development Editor: Gemma Cary

Editor: Suzanne Adams

Assistant Editor: Alex Albrighton

Series Designer: Anna Oliwa

Designer: Liz Gilbert

Cover Image: Jill Murphy

Illustrations: Jill Murphy and Mike Phillips/Beehive Illustration

Text © 2010 Celia Warren   © 2010 Scholastic Ltd

Designed using Adobe InDesign

Published by Scholastic Ltd,
Book End, Range Road, Witney,
Oxfordshire OX29 0YD
www.scholastic.co.uk

Printed by Bell & Bain
123456789   0123456789

British Library Cataloguing-in-Publication Data
A catalogue record for this book is available from
the British Library.
ISBN 978-1407-11865-9

Acknowledgements

The publishers gratefully acknowledge permission to reproduce the following copyright material: **Pamela Todd** for the use of an illustration from *The Worst Witch* by Jill Murphy © 1974, Jill Murphy (1974, Allison & Busby). **Penguin Group Ltd** for the use of the front cover, text and illustrations from *The Worst Witch* by Jill Murphy © 1974, Jill Murphy (1978, Puffin).
Every effort has been made to trace copyright holders for the works reproduced in this book, and the publishers apologise for any inadvertent omissions.

The Worst Witch

About the book

First published in 1974, this delightful story, the first of a series, features the accident-prone but well-meaning character, Mildred Hubble. The young witch and her friends receive a traditional British school education with a magical twist. In Miss Cackle's Academy for Witches' readers encounter classic magical components drawn from all the best children's perceptions of witches, from cats and cauldrons to broomsticks and potions. The setting is an isolated mountain-top castle and the time of year, of course, is Hallowe'en.

The story embraces old-fashioned icons of British schooling, such as the ubiquitous gymslip and tie, timetables and tests, homework and the looming of distant exams (Higher Witches' Certificate). Readers recognise the archetypal teacher's pet, Ethel (with a bossiness that borders on bullying); the strict-but-fair form mistress, Miss Hardbroom; the kind-hearted headteacher, Miss Cackle; and the reliable best friend, Maud.

Mildred quickly endears herself to the reader with her openness, vulnerability, often-thwarted effort and latent clumsiness, all of which seem exacerbated by her bad luck. She resignedly accepts ownership of the only tabby kitten when the school runs out of black ones, along with the inevitable breaking of her only broom by accident.

Her decision to run away rather than face the music over an incident which is not her fault, and the subsequent discovery that provides her with the means to save the school from takeover by wicked witches, bring the story to a satisfying conclusion.

En route, the gentle humour is a delight and includes casual comments offered with the author's typical light touch, such as when Mildred leaves the room and exhorts her kitten not to tease the bats.

Despite the simplicity of this straightforward adventure, told across ten chapters, there is much scope for discussion of personal goals and achievement, aspirations and disappointments, and issues such as dealing with bullies and being true to oneself. It is a modern fairy tale in an old-school setting, inviting ready empathy.

About the author

Jill Murphy was born in London in 1949 and loved storytelling from an early age, spending much of her childhood writing and illustrating her own children's stories. After leaving school, she attended Chelsea Art School and Croydon Art School. She illustrates her own books and began writing the stories about Mildred Hubble when she was 16 and still at school herself. She was 24 when *The Worst Witch* was published. Children reading *The Worst Witch* may recall colourful picture books, written and illustrated by the same author, including *Peace at Last* and *Five Minutes' Peace*, about the popular Large family of elephants.

> ### Facts and figures
> *The Worst Witch* is the first of a series of six books about Mildred Hubble and her friends. In 1986 it was made into a television series. Jill Murphy's work has won her numerous prizes and awards, including the Kate Greenaway Medal for *Peace at Last*, the Best Books for Babies Award for *Five Minutes' Peace*, and the Smarties Book Prize for *The Last Noo-noo*.

Guided reading

Chapter One

The first chapter sets the scene – a dark, isolated castle on a mountain, black hats and broomsticks, bats, owls and potions – and introduces the main characters, whose names echo with magical connotations, such as Mildred Hubble and Miss Cackle (the head of the Witches' Academy). The name of Mildred's form teacher, Miss Hardbroom, adds a clue to her character, too. Readers learn about Mildred's appearance and personality, in contrast to her best friend Maud's. For example, things tend to go wrong for Mildred and surprisingly, for a witch, she is afraid of the dark. She also has a habit of chewing her plaits. Ask the children if they have any nervous habits like Mildred's.

Miss Cackle's Academy for Witches is renowned for being traditional. Discuss punishments such as *writing lines* and *being kept in*. Ensure that the children understand that *lab* is an abbreviation and discuss what lessons would take place in a laboratory. Ask: *Why do Mildred's friends choose to* keep their distance in the lab? What activities have the children in your class learned that help them identify with Mildred's difficulty in learning to ride a broom? (For example: learning to ride a bike, scooter or roller skates.) Explain *new-fangled nonsense* – non-traditional teaching methods. Briefly discuss what might be considered new-fangled, such as the use of computers and touch-screen whiteboards, less learning by rote, and so on.

Chapter Two

The second chapter opens with the exciting event of the presentation of the kittens, only for Mildred to be singled out as the only girl not to receive the traditional black kitten. Discuss the aspirational and emotive words of the school song. Ask: *What does the word* droning *suggest about the pupils' feelings? Why do the supposedly stirring words not appear to motivate the young witches?* Point out the narrator's voice as she addresses the reader directly with lines such as *as I have mentioned before.*

Ensure that the children understand the meaning of *literally* in reference to Miss Hardbroom's disappearance. Explore the ways we use *disappear* in everyday contexts with a non-literal, metaphorical meaning – for example, *My book's disappeared* meaning *I can't find my book*, or *It's time for me to disappear* meaning *I have to go now.*

Study the illustrations and talk about how they add an extra dimension to the story. Point out that the author is also the illustrator, so she has total control over the pictures she wants to put across in both words and drawings.

Chapter Three

Ask the children: *How does inserting the word* certain *affect the meaning of the line* a certain young witch called Ethel? *How does it influence the reader's feelings about the character? What warning message does it relay?* Explain how the addition of that one small word helps readers to 'read between the lines' and warns them that there's more to Ethel than immediately meets the eye.

As a class, define the terms *protagonist* and *antagonist* in terms of Mildred Hubble and Ethel Hallow: Mildred the heroine, leading role and friendly central character versus Ethel, chief rival, adversary and enemy.

Discuss the description of Ethel as one of those lucky people for whom everything goes right and how it is implied that, because Ethel is clever, she thinks it gives her the right to be bossy to her peers. Can the children relate to how the inept and unfortunate Mildred might find her annoying?

Encourage the children to examine how Ethel goads Mildred into acting in anger. Are they surprised when Mildred's spell to turn Ethel into a frog goes wrong? Why not? (Recap on the many clues as to Mildred's tendency to make mistakes.) From the context, can the children discern the meaning of the metaphorical expression *That's torn it?* Invite them to compare the sentence that follows: *You've done it now, Mildred!* Challenge the children to rephrase *it is not customary…* in less formal language such as *we don't usually…*

Ask: *Why does Mildred remind Ethel of the silence rule in the library? How might she benefit from Ethel's silence?* (It deflects Ethel from expressing her anger and avoids an embarrassing scene.)

Chapter Four

Invite the children to describe what *filing in* means, as the young witches enter the potion laboratory for their test. Explain how the use of hyphens in *pondweed-gathered-at-midnight* turns the four separate words into one term or name for the ingredient. List the children's suggestions for events that might be described as emergencies requiring the use of a laughter potion. Point out how the author uses this unlikely coupling for humour in the instruction that *a laughter potion should be made quickly for use in an emergency.*

Ask why Miss Cackle's being sad and disappointed rather than angry could make Mildred feel about an inch high, and what this reveals about Mildred's feelings and Miss Cackle's. (Mildred does not mean to disappoint her teachers and Miss Cackle recognises that her mistakes are unintentional, feeling exasperated rather than cross.)

Chapter Five

Ask the children what the term *shot a glance* means and encourage the children to practise this with a friend. Ask: *Why did Miss Hardbroom glance at Mildred at that moment in her speech? What might have been worrying the teacher?* Discuss what a broomstick formation team might do. Compare the broomstick formation team with other formation activities such as the Red Arrows flying displays, synchronised swimming and dancing events. List the verbs that help convey the noisy excitement as the girls collect their brooms and head outside: *clattered, rushed, rang.* Ensure that the children understand the line *Form an orderly crocodile.* Finally, draw attention to the narrator's direct assertion that Ethel really wasn't a nice person at all.

Chapter Six

As the children begin reading this chapter, encourage them to look closely at the illustration of the silhouetted witches. Can they guess which witch is Mildred? (The one whose bootlace has come undone.) Discuss how illustrations complement the text by conveying the written word but also adding unwritten information. Discuss why Miss Cackle closed her eyes during the low-flying part of the display.

Chapter Seven

Mildred and the others return to school at dawn. No one is speaking to Mildred as she takes the blame for the disastrous display. Mildred dreads facing her teacher and headmistress in the office the following day, and Ethel crows over her misfortune, revealing that she had bewitched the loaned broom. Point out how speech marks are used to indicate Mildred's thoughts, her 'inner dialogue'. Can the children recognise the rhetorical nature of Mildred's questions? Discuss how far ahead Mildred planned her escape and how she must have felt as she set off. Check the children understand the idea of being in disgrace, and know the meaning of the terms *picture rail* and *expel.*

Chapter Eight

The end of the previous chapter and this chapter reach a pivotal point in the story. It is the point at which Mildred feels most despairing, ill-treated and unloved. Discuss Mildred's feelings and ask the children if they would seek revenge on Ethel (as Ethel did on Mildred after the pig-transformation). Alert the children to Mildred's first thoughts when she overhears the wicked witches' plotting. She knows she must stop it and thinks, firstly, of her friend Maud. List some of the qualities revealed by Mildred's behaviour: *loyalty, duty, obligation, care* and *responsibility.*

Draw attention to the description of how the noise gradually impinges on Mildred as she works out what and where it's coming from. Ask the children to explain how Mildred justifies breaking the Witches' Code before turning the plotting witches into snails. Point out how the description is made more graphic by added details, such as the difficulty of waving her arms in a circle towards the very people she is hiding from. Note the use of the two Ms (Mildred and Maud) emphasising that the reader knows them well.

Chapter Nine

Challenge the children to demonstrate the possible facial expressions of Miss Hardbroom that show she disbelieves Mildred's story about the snails. (For example, raised eyebrows, pinched lips, slow-blinking eyes, eyes cast up.)

Can the children imagine why the Witches' Code should need so many paragraphs (rule seven, paragraph five)? Explain that the same is true of a country's laws.

Encourage the children to examine how the author shows that Miss Hardbroom is suspicious over Mildred's being out alone at night, through the character's sarcastic statements and questions. (For example: *I suppose these are the witches? And I expect you were also singing the school song as you rambled along, weren't you, my dear?*)

Chapter Ten

Ask the children if they think justice has been done, as Ethel's mean trick is exposed, without Mildred's having told tales on her. As she is applauded in front of the whole school, identify all the ways in which modest Mildred's embarrassment is shown in the description of events: *went bright red, stumbled, tripping, clumped, blushed, twisted her fingers behind her back.*

As the story is rounded off, ask the children how differently they feel about Miss Hardbroom at the end of the story, compared with at the beginning. Discuss why their opinions might have been modified. Can they identify at what point in the story a softer side to Miss Hardbroom began to show (perhaps when she is flying with her hair loose, looking less threatening)? Invite the children to laugh with Miss Hardbroom at the close of the story and note how the ending lends itself to a sequel.

Shared reading

Extract 1

● Highlight the layout of dialogue in the first extract – for example, punctuation, indentation and variety of direct-speech tag words such as *confessed, said, inquired, continued, chorused.*

● Ring the adverbs that modify tag words and actions: *nastily, icily, miserably, (glared) meaningfully, hastily (blew).* Discuss how these help readers to visualise the characters and accentuate characters' feelings.

● Ring the italicised words, *Some*thing and *witch* and then read aloud the sentences in which they appear, adding extra stress to the italicised parts, to show how font format guides readers as to the author's intention.

● Examine the rhetorical nature of Miss Hardbroom's question and what it conveys to the girls, as well as her use of the first-person pronoun *we*. Ask: *How does this belittle the girls?* (It is condescending and patronising.)

● Highlight effective verbs, comparing their emotive quality alongside simpler verbs. For example, compare *leap (out of the window)* with the verb *jump*; compare *(black hair) scragged back* with *brushed back*; compare *Miss Hardbroom glared* with *looked*; compare *dived (under the bedclothes)* with *hid*.

Extract 2

● Examine how the excitement and celebration builds up through detailed attention to sequenced actions. List the stages of Mildred's preparation (*1. Smoothes robes, 2. Says good-bye to kitten, 3. Puts on her hat* and so on).

● Ask: *How might Class One feel as the youngest and newest participants?* Consider the evidence, such as, they are the last class to set off; they are the only class without cats (as they are still only kittens); they've never seen Miss Hardbroom in her festive robes and with loose hair before now.

● Discuss which aspects of the text show the girls' increasing familiarity with the school. For example, underline *H.B.*, their nickname for Miss Hardbroom.

● Draw attention to Miss Hardbroom's reprimand to Mildred's and Maud's whispered conversation, which immediately puts them in their place as the youngest, most inexperienced participants of the Hallowe'en celebrations.

● Encourage the children to compare the illustration with the text. Although the characters are in silhouette, how can the children recognise Miss Hardbroom, Mildred and Maud?

Extract 3

● Underline the girls' traditional response to Miss Cackle's arrival, *Everyone stood up.* Ask: *Do children still do this today when someone important walks into a room?* (Perhaps every day at school or at special gatherings.) Discuss why people sometimes stand when someone important walks in. (It is a display of respect.)

● Highlight the use of the word *certain* (*a certain young member of the school*). Explain how this singles out Mildred for distinction and merit. Compare the word's use in Chapter Three: *a certain young witch named Ethel* – also distinguishing the character from others, but instead for negative behaviour.

● Underline all the sentences and phrases that describe Mildred's embarrassment before the word is actually used. Ask how Miss Cackle's words imply Mildred's apparent discomfort and then circle *don't be shy.*

● Highlight the use of quotation marks around *the heroine*. Ask why they are used (to indicate that Mildred is a reluctant recipient of the title).

Extract 1

From Chapter One

'I'm worried about the whole thing,' Mildred confessed, chewing the end of her plait. 'I'm sure I'll do something dreadful like treading on its tail, or else it'll take one look at me and leap out of the window. *Some*thing's bound to go wrong.'

'Don't be silly,' said Maud. 'You know you have a way with animals. And as for treading on its tail, it won't even be on the floor. Miss Cackle hands it to you, and that's all there is to it. So there's nothing to worry about, is there?'

Before Mildred had time to reply, the door crashed open to reveal their form-mistress Miss Hardbroom standing in the doorway wrapped in a black dressing-gown, with a lantern in her hand. She was a tall, terrifying lady, with a sharp, bony face and black hair scragged back into such a tight knot that her forehead looked quite stretched.

'Rather late to be up, isn't it girls?' she inquired nastily.

The girls, who had leapt into each other's arms when the door burst open, drew apart and fixed their eyes on the floor.

'Of course, if we don't want to be included in the presentation tomorrow we are certainly going about it the right way,' Miss Hardbroom continued icily.

'Yes, Miss Hardbroom,' chorused the girls miserably.

Miss Hardbroom glared meaningfully at Mildred's candle and swept out into the corridor with Maud in front of her.

Mildred hastily blew out the candle and dived under the bedclothes, but she could not get to sleep. Outside the window she could hear the owls hooting, and somewhere in the school a door had been left open and was creaking backwards and forwards in the wind. To tell you the truth, Mildred was afraid of the dark, but don't tell anyone. I mean, whoever heard of a *witch* who was scared of the dark?

Text © 1974, Jill Murphy

Extract 2

From Chapter Six

As the sun set, the members of Miss Cackle's Academy were preparing to leave the school. Mildred smoothed her robes, said good-bye to her kitten, put on her hat, grabbed Ethel's broomstick and ran down to the yard. She took a quick look out of her window before leaving the room and saw the fires being lit in the distance. It was very exciting.

The rest of the school had already assembled as Mildred rushed out of the door and took her place. Miss Hardbroom looked splendid in her full witch's robes and hat.

'Everyone is present now,' Miss Hardbroom announced to Miss Cackle.

'Then we shall set off,' said the headmistress. 'To the celebrations! Class Five first, Class Four second, and so on until Class One!'

They made a wonderful sight flying over the trees towards the castle, cloaks soaring in the wind, and the older girls with their cats perched on the ends of their broomsticks. Miss Hardbroom looked particularly impressive, sitting bolt-upright with her long black hair streaming behind her. The girls had never seen her hair loose before and were amazed how much of it she could possibly scrag into that tight knot every day. It came down to her waist.

'H.B. looks quite nice with her hair like that,' whispered Maud to Mildred, who was riding next to her.

'Yes,' agreed Mildred, 'she doesn't seem half as frightening.'

Miss Hardbroom turned round and shot a piercing look at the two girls.

'No talking!' she snapped.

Text and illustrations © 1974, Jill Murphy.

Extract 3

From Chapter Ten

'You may sit down, girls,' said the headmistress. 'As you all know, the school narrowly escaped invasion this morning. Had it not been for a certain young member of the school we should not be here but would be hopping about turned into frogs.'

The girls laughed.

'No, no, girls! Do not laugh! It would not be at all funny had it happened. However, as it did *not* happen, I proclaim the rest of today a half holiday in honour of Mildred Hubble. Mildred, would you come up here for a moment?'

Mildred went bright red and was pushed to her feet. She stumbled through the rows of chairs, tripping over feet as she went, and clumped across the platform to Miss Cackle's table.

'Now don't be shy, my dear,' said Miss Cackle beaming. She turned to the school. 'Come along, school! Three cheers for our heroine Mildred.'

Mildred blushed and twisted her fingers behind her back as the cheers rang out.

It was a relief to 'the heroine' when it was all over. As they filed out of the hall, she was thumped on the back and congratulated by everyone – except for Ethel who gave Mildred the nastiest look you've ever seen.

'Good old Mil!' yelled someone.

'We'll get out of our chanting test, thanks to you,' said someone else.

'Thanks for the holiday!'

'Thanks, Mil!' And so on.

Maud flung an arm around her friend.

'You did look embarrassed,' she said. 'You went ever so red, I could see you from the back of the hall!'

'Oh, *don't*,' said Mildred. 'Let's go and fetch the kittens and make the most of our holiday.'

Text © 1974, Jill Murphy

Plot, character and setting

Fact file

> **Objective:** To identify and make notes on the main points of a section of text.
> **What you need:** Copies of *The Worst Witch*, photocopiable page 15, enlarged copy of Extract 1, writing materials.
> **Cross-curricular link:** Art and design.

What to do

● Ask the children to read the first chapter of the book or read it together as a class.
● Invite the children to sum up briefly the content and purpose of the chapter. (To establish the setting and introduce the main characters and to intimate the tone of the story, creating expectations and curiosity in the reader's mind.)
● Ask: *What does it mean to have a way with animals?* (To respond well to animals, understanding their nature, so that animals instinctively trust and like you, and come to you readily.)

● Display Extract 1 and re-read it with the class, underlining anything that tells us about Mildred's looks, habits, personality and behaviour. For example: *worried; chewing…plait; best friend Maud; scared of the dark.*
● Hand out copies of photocopiable page 15 and invite the children to re-read Chapter One, making notes to create a 'Mildred Hubble fact file' based on information in that first chapter. (NB The school badge is described early in the chapter.)

> **Differentiation**
> **For older/more confident learners:** Ask the children to write about whether they would be friends with Mildred, if they were in her class. Encourage them to give reasons.
> **For younger/less confident learners:** Invite the children to underline anything about themselves that they have in common with Mildred, such as being scared of the dark.

I know what it's like!

> **Objective:** To identify features that writers use to provoke readers' reactions.
> **What you need:** Copies of *The Worst Witch*, writing materials.

What to do

● Re-read the narrator's plea to the reader at the close of Chapter One: *…don't tell anyone. I mean, whoever heard of a witch who was afraid of the dark?* Ask the children: *Can you find another example of the narrator addressing the reader in Chapter Two?* (*Riding a broomstick was no easy matter, as I have mentioned before.*) Discuss how this affects the reader's response to Mildred. (It makes them like her/feel sorry for her.)
● Read from *The difficult part was balancing…* to *…until a friend came to your rescue* (Chapter Two). Does it remind the children of when they

learned a skill, such as riding a bike or a pony? Share some of their experiences.
● Ask: *How does Miss Hardbroom later imply a similarity to riding a bike?* (*…possibly it would be even easier with handlebars and a saddle.*) Point out the adjective *icy* and Mildred's blushing. Ask: *What tone of voice has the teacher adopted that makes Mildred blush?* (Sarcastic and patronising.) *What effect do the teacher's comments have on the reader?* (They help the reader to identify with Mildred's struggles and feel sympathetic towards her.)

> **Differentiation**
> **For older/more confident learners:** Challenge the children to write a dialogue based on their own experience of learning a new skill.
> **For younger/less confident learners:** Ask children to work in pairs or small groups to find more examples of the narrator directly addressing the reader.

Plot, character and setting

Out of context

Objective: To identify and summarise evidence from a text to support a hypothesis.
What you need: Copies of *The Worst Witch*, writing materials, photocopiable page 16.
Cross curricular link: PSHE.

What to do

● Read to the end of Chapter Three and discuss why Mildred put a spell on Ethel. Ask: *Was it reasonable? Understandable? Justifiable? Unkind? Did it please Mildred when Ethel turned into a pig? Did she gloat?* Make sure the children explain their opinions, with reference to the text.

● Hand out copies of photocopiable page 16. Explain that the quotations are 'taken out of context' and what this means; some of them have been abridged and so do not give the full picture. Ask the children to find the quotations in Chapter Three and read around them, checking what has

just happened and what events follow.

● When writing their answers, encourage the children to quote directly from the book to support their opinions. Share their findings as a whole class.

● Discuss how Ethel's taunting makes Mildred react. (*Go* on, *then, if you're so clever.* Turn *me into a frog!*) Ask: *How might Mildred have responded in a wiser way? If Mildred had ignored her or only retaliated verbally, would that have made a good story?* Establish that interesting stories need protagonists, antagonists and conflict.

Differentiation
For older/more confident learners: Challenge the children to list quotations that support the narrator's statement that Ethel really wasn't a nice person at all.
For younger/less confident learners: Allow the children to work in pairs locating the quotations, with the more confident writer acting as scribe.

Dramatic words

Objective: To explore how writers use language for dramatic effect.
What you need: Copies of *The Worst Witch*, dictionaries, a whiteboard, an enlarged copy of Extract 2, highlighter pen.

What to do

● List the words: *soar, perch, stream, shoot, pierce* and *snap.*

● Challenge the children to write a sentence for each verb, which shows its meaning. Point out that they may add the suffixes '-ed' or '-ing' (or use past tense *shot*) if they wish.

● Share two or three sentences for each verb, and agree definitions for them. Invite the children to use dictionaries and amend the definitions accordingly.

● Explain that these verbs are used in Chapter Six of *The Worst Witch* and read the first paragraph of the chapter aloud.

● Display Extract 2 and read aloud, asking children to put up their hands when you reach one of the listed verbs, such as *cloaks soaring in the wind.* Highlight each verb. Point out that, here, *piercing* is used as an adjective.

● Invite the children to offer a simpler synonym for each verb, such as *flying* (for *soaring*), *sitting* (for *perched*), *flowing* (for *streaming*). Invite children to comment on why the original words work best. (For example, *streaming* suggests speed and a constant, determined direction of movement.)

Differentiation
For older/more confident learners: Challenge the children to find further strong, evocative verbs. Share, compare and discuss their findings.
For younger/less confident learners: Ask the children to copy the six sentences containing the highlighted words and underline the verbs.

Plot, character and setting

When time slows down

> **Objective:** To deduce characters' reasons for behaviour.
> **What you need:** Copies of *The Worst Witch*.
> **Cross-curricular link:** PSHE.

What to do

● When the children have read to the end of Chapter Seven, invite them to explain why Mildred decides to run away. (Feelings of guilt; worry about meeting the Headmistress; possible punishment.)

● Ask: *Why does Mildred decide to leave there and then? What comforts her and what does she think she will miss when she has left?*

● Remind the children that between Chapters One and Two, half a school term has passed. Ask: *How long has passed in Chapter Seven?* (Two hours.) *Does two hours awake in bed seem longer than two hours up and busy? Why?*

● Challenge the children to list, in sequence, all the thoughts that go through Mildred's mind in those two hours.

● Invite the children to discuss which factors most influence Mildred's decision to run away, using quotations to support their opinions.

● Ask why the teachers do not deal with Mildred's mishap straight away. Would it have been easier for Mildred if they had?

> **Differentiation**
> **For older/more confident learners:** Ask the children to discuss why they think Mildred does not tell about Ethel's unkind trick, and if they think she is right not to. Ask: *When should someone tell a teacher about another child's unkindness?* (When they are being bullied or if there is a safety issue involved.)
> **For younger/less confident learners:** Ask the children to explain in their own words why Mildred felt reassured that she would not be turned into a frog.

Speaking and thinking

> **Objective:** To compare the usefulness of techniques such as visualisation, prediction and empathy.
> **What you need:** Copies of *The Worst Witch*, enlarged copies of photocopiable page 17.

What to do

● The only company Mildred has, in Chapters Seven and Eight, is Tabby. Sometimes she talks to the kitten and sometimes the reader 'hears' her thinking. Point out how both her speech and thoughts are in speech marks. Discuss why. (To emphasise dialogue and inner dialogue.)

● Hand out copies of photocopiable page 17. Ask the children to add more direct quotations from Chapters Seven and Eight, in the speech bubble when Mildred is speaking aloud, and in the thought bubble when they are inner dialogue.

Point out how inner dialogue and speaking aloud can both reveal the character's decision-making process.

● Ask the children to leave out any tag words, such as *said*, and only write the words that are direct speech or thought.

> **Differentiation**
> **For older/more confident learners:** Challenge the children to explain in a paragraph, why authors use inner dialogue in their narrative. (It makes it easier for the reader to empathise with the character's feelings and follow her train of thought and to imagine and predict her plans.)
> **For younger/less confident learners:** Write relevant quotations on small cards for the children to locate in the book, sort and copy into the speech and thought bubbles.

Plot, character and setting

Showing feelings

> **Objective:** To infer characters' feelings in fiction and consequences in logical explanations.
> **What you need:** Copies of *The Worst Witch*, enlarged copy of Extract 3.
> **Cross-curricular link:** PSHE.

What to do

● Display Extract 3, first obscuring the word *embarrassed* in the penultimate section. Read the extract aloud to the class, as far as *Maud flung an arm around her friend*, asking the children to focus their attention on the descriptions of Mildred's behaviour and reactions.

● List the behavioural clues that indicate how Mildred feels: *went bright red*; *was pushed to her feet*; *stumbled*; *tripping*; *clumped*; *blushed*; *twisted her fingers behind her back*; *relief… when it was all over*.

● Return to the extract and ask the children if they can predict (or remember) the missing word *embarrassed*. Even if they did not recall it, ask what clues imply embarrassment.

● Reveal the obscured word. Ask which verb, used earlier, means *to go red* (blush). Challenge the children to explain what Mildred means by *Oh, don't!* Can they suggest how that exclamation might be completed?

> **Differentiation**
> **For older/more confident learners:** Ask the children to consider how Maud must feel during this scene. Ask: *Is she proud, anxious, keen to make amends for doubting Mildred, amused at Mildred's embarrassment?* Discuss why Maud flung an arm around her friend. What does this gesture indicate?
> **For younger/less confident learners:** Invite the children to retell this incident to a partner, in the first person, past tense, as Mildred. You could provide the relevant quotations as a prompt. Encourage partners to discuss Mildred's feelings.

In a nutshell

> **Objective:** To make notes of the main points in sections of text.
> **What you need:** Copies of *The Worst Witch*, photocopiable page 18, scissors, glue, spare plain paper (optional).
> **Cross curricular link:** Art and design.

What to do

● After reading the book, observe how the story is divided into ten chapters. Discuss the purpose of chapters, as broadly as possible. (Easily digestible chunks; means of moving from scene to scene, making a jump in time or focusing on different characters or relationships.)

● Point out that every chapter links to the previous and following chapters, developing the plot and rounding the characters.

● Explain how even apparently unimportant descriptions serve a purpose. For example: the account of Miss Cackle's physical appearance and green glasses is significant for later when Mildred spots her 'double' who turns out to be her wicked sister Agatha. *The Popular Book of Spells* is important as Mildred takes this with her when she runs away. Invite further examples.

● Hand out copies of photocopiable page 18. Clarify the meaning of the expression *in a nutshell*. (Short and concise, containing the most important bits.) Ask the children to complete the activity, telling them you will look for accurate identification of main plot events, clearly expressed and in their own words.

> **Differentiation**
> **For older/more confident learners:** Challenge the children to write a succinct account of the whole plot of the book, on one side of A4 paper.
> **For younger/less confident learners:** Enlarge the photocopiable sheet. Working in pairs, ask children to cut out and sequence the chapter summaries.

Plot, character and setting

Fact file

● Use the information in Chapter 1 to help you complete Mildred's fact file.

Name: _Mildred Hubble_ _____

School: _____

Form-mistress: _____

Mildred's appearance: _____

_____

Best friend: _____

Nervous habit: _____

Likely to achieve an award for: _____

_____

School badge:

Plot, character and setting

Out of context

● Below are some quotations from Chapter 3. They are taken out of context, and some are incomplete, but they appear to support the view that Mildred is mean, unkind and spiteful.

● Read each quotation and decide whether it supports this view. Explain why, putting the quotation in context to support your opinion.

1. 'I shall have to turn you into a frog…'

_____

_____

_____

2. Mildred muttered the spell under her breath – and Ethel vanished.

_____

_____

_____

3. 'Oh, stop going on!' said Mildred… 'It's all your fault…'

_____

_____

_____

4. Mildred ignored the grunting Ethel…

_____

_____

_____

SECTION
4

Speaking and thinking

● Scan Chapters Seven and Eight of *The Worst Witch*, looking for Mildred's speech marks.

● Choose some quotations to write below, putting Mildred's speech in the speech bubble, and her thoughts in the thought bubble.

● Note the chapter and page numbers alongside.

Plot, character and setting

In a nutshell

● Match the main events to each chapter, and write the correct chapter number in the box. One is done for you.

● Write your own brief summary of each of the last five chapters.

Chapter	Mildred's laughter potion goes wrong, making her and Maud disappear. Mildred has to go and see the Headmistress.
Chapter 1	The main characters are introduced and the setting of Miss Cackle's Academy for Witches, is described.
Chapter	Ethel mocks Mildred and challenges her to turn her into a frog. Mildred tries to do so, but turns Ethel into a pig.
Chapter	Miss Hardbroom starts a broomstick formation team. Ethel lends Mildred her spare broom, but enchants it first.
Chapter	Kittens are presented to Mildred's class. All are black except for Mildred's tabby. The girls learn how to ride broomsticks.
Chapter 6	
Chapter 7	
Chapter 8	
Chapter 9	
Chapter 10	

Talk about it

Too excited to sleep

> **Objective:** To use and recognise the impact of theatrical effects in drama.
> **What you need:** Copies of *The Worst Witch*, photocopiable page 22, an enlarged copy of Extract 1.
> **Cross-curricular link:** Drama.

What to do

● Hand out copies of photocopiable page 22. Explain that this is an incomplete playscript. Ask the children to find Maud and Mildred's dialogue in Chapter One. Ask: *How does the script layout differ from the layout in the book? What is the significance of italics and brackets?*

● Ask the class to think about who will say what next, with reference to the original text.

● Highlight the direct speech in Extract 1, using different colours for different characters. Point out how tag words and description outside of the speech marks are not words spoken by characters. The surrounding narrative can be useful for stage directions in brackets. For example: (*Mildred chews her plait, nervously*).

● Tell the children, working in small groups, to complete the script of the scene.

● When their scripts are complete, invite the children to choose a role each. Ask them, initially, to practise doing a simple script-reading, as if for radio, concentrating on variation of tone, volume and pace.

● Later, invite the children to act out the scene using facial expression and gesture.

> **Differentiation**
> **For older/more confident learners:** Challenge the children to add sound effects (approaching footsteps, creaking door, owl hooting). Encourage them to learn their lines off by heart.
> **For younger/less confident learners:** Help the children word-process their scripts, and print out three copies with roles colour-coded for easy identification.

Poetry and prose

> **Objective:** To compare how a common theme is presented in poetry and prose.
> **What you need:** Copies of *The Worst Witch*, handwritten copies of the school song from Chapter Two.

What to do

● When the children have read at least the first four chapters, read in chorus the Witches' Academy school song from Chapter Two.

● Quote the narrator's observation: …*usual type of school song, full of pride, joy and striving.* Invite the children to identify evidence of these three aspects.

● Discuss the purpose of a school song (to inspire, motivate, evoke loyalty).

● Ask groups of children to discuss and make notes on how the teachers' expectations reflect the words of the song and how far the pupils live up to its sentiments. (Encourage them to look closely at Mildred and Ethel, Miss Hardbroom and Miss Cackle.)

● Invite each group to present their findings, with evidence from the text. Discuss why Academy life falls short of the song's aspirations. Ask: *Why does poetry lend itself better to the song, and prose to the story?*

> **Differentiation**
> **For older/more confident learners:** When the children are further through the book, return to this discussion about the teachers' expectations and how far the children live up to them. Talk about whether the children have altered their inferences and opinions about the teachers and pupils.
> **For younger/less confident learners:** Ask: *How did the pupils sing the song?* (They were droning.) *What does this suggest?* Children can find examples of events that do and don't fulfil the song's aspirations.

Talk about it

Group formation

Objective: To plan and manage a group task over time using different levels of planning.
What you need: Copies of *The Worst Witch*, the cardboard tube of a kitchen roll (one for each child, if available), a large space (such as the hall or playground).
Cross-curricular links: Drama, dance/PE.

What to do
● Ask the children to read Chapters Five and Six. Together, list the sequence of four manoeuvres forming the witches' broomstick formation team's display (sinking and rising alternately; a flying V-formation; nose-diving and quickly swooping up again; forming a circle).
● Take the children into a large space and ask them to practise emulating these moves, on their feet, as if sitting on a broomstick. Use cardboard tubes to represent broom-handles.
● Sort the children into groups to discuss, devise and practise a short new display. They may incorporate ideas from the book but should add one or two new manoeuvres (such as: a double-crocodile, 'fly' out and away from their partner to u-turn back and reform the crocodile; a zig-zag from side to side).
● Watch each display and invite groups to hold up marks out of ten for each performance at the end. (They can hold up their fingers to score, allowing no fewer than three points to be awarded for any display.)

Differentiation
For older/more confident learners: Invite a member of each group to introduce their team and commentate during their display.
For younger/less confident learners: Provide a set of commentary-style phrases for children to adapt. (*And Jones performs a swoop! It's a successful double crocodile by Smith!*)

First impressions

Objective: To follow up others' points and show whether they agree or disagree in whole-class discussion.
What you need: Copies of *The Worst Witch*, photocopiable page 23.

What to do
● Ask the children to think about when they met someone for the first time, and to consider their first impressions. Ask: *Did you instantly like the person? Did you have doubts that were proved either right or wrong? Did you change your mind after getting to know them better? Why?*
● Discuss Mildred's and Miss Hardbroom's opinions of each other throughout the book. Note the words used to describe their relationship (*afraid, in awe, respectful, disdainful, angry, exasperated*). Ask: *Does Mildred's opinion of 'H.B.' change more than the other way round?*
● Hand out copies of photocopiable page 23. Allow the children ten minutes to read through the quotations and discuss the questions briefly with a partner.
● Open the discussion to the whole class, encouraging listeners to support or question speakers, and explain their agreement or disagreement.

Differentiation
For older/more confident learners: Ask: *To whom does Miss Hardbroom's behaviour most drastically change over the course of the story? Why?* (Compare and discuss her manner towards Ethel in Chapters Three, Five and Ten.)
For younger/less confident learners: Help the children find the quotations, and then explain the events that might affect the two characters' reactions to each other. Ask, for example: *Why is Mildred afraid of Miss Hardbroom and not of Miss Cackle?*

Talk about it

News team

> **Objective:** To identify different question types and evaluate their impact on the audience.
> **What you need:** Copies of *The Worst Witch*, photocopiable page 24, props such as microphones (optional).
> **Cross-curricular link:** Drama.

What to do

● Ask the children to imagine how the narrowly averted school takeover might be reported on television news.
● Who might the reporters want to interview – Miss Cackle, Mildred? List question words such as *why, where, how, when, which* and *who*. Together, compile some open-ended questions (requiring more than a *yes* or *no* answer).
● Offer examples of leading questions, where the reporter is implying certain angles or making assumptions, such as: *How upset were you, Mildred? How angry were your teachers?*
● Divide the class into groups to role play a television news report, with leading characters being interviewed by reporters 'on location' (outside the wizard's court, at the school, in the forest) and 'in the studio'.
● Hand out copies of photocopiable page 24 so the children can plan their news reports. Watch each group present their news item and invite constructive feedback from the class.

> **Differentiation**
> **For older/more confident learners:** Ask the children to analyse the success of each performance, commenting on how informative it was and the reporter's stance.
> **For younger/less confident learners:** Act as scribe for the group's questions, and encourage them to consider possible responses from the reporters, who will respond without a script.

Contrasts

> **Objective:** To use drama strategies to explore stories or issues.
> **What you need:** Copies of *The Worst Witch*.
> **Cross-curricular links:** Drama, PSHE.

What to do

● Ask the children to compare the situations Mildred finds herself in after the Hallowe'en disaster (Chapter Seven), and after the announcement of the half-day holiday (Chapter Ten).
● Ask: *What is the main difference between the attitudes of others towards Mildred?* List contrasting, contradictory words, such as *blame, anger, disgust* and *praise, delight, admiration*.
● Ask the children to imagine they are Mildred. Address them first as *Mildred*, then *Mildred Hubble*, then *Mil*, adjusting tone of voice appropriately. Listen to individuals describing their inferences and different feelings.
● Pick a volunteer to role play Mildred. Divide the class into two lines facing each other, role playing Mildred's classmates. Ask 'Mildred' to walk between the two lines, while those on the left call out insulting jeers, both quoted and invented. As 'Mildred' turns to walk back, those on the right call out congratulatory, admiring phrases. Can 'Mildred' describe and compare her feelings as she walked along each line?

> **Differentiation**
> **For older/more confident learners:** Challenge the children in pairs to role play as Mildred and Maud. Begin with Maud telling Mildred how she felt on each of these two occasions, with Mildred responding.
> **For younger/less confident learners:** Write out some speeches as 'call-out' prompts for children to practise and learn, such as *You're so clumsy, Hubble!* and *Well done, Mil!* before attempting the whole-class role-play exercise.

Talk about it

Too excited to sleep

● Continue this script and include stage directions.

A playscript based on a scene from the opening chapter of The Worst Witch by Jill Murphy.

Setting: *Mildred's bedroom in a dark castle. Bats are hanging upside down from the picture rail. Mildred is in bed when her friend Maud creeps in. A candle is burning beside her bed.*

Narrator: It was the night before the presentation of kittens to new pupils at Miss Cackle's Academy for Witches. Maud was too excited to sleep…

Mildred: (yawning) What are you going to call your kitten, Maud?

Maud: Midnight. I think it sounds dramatic.

Mildred:

Illustrations © 2010, Mike Phillips/Beehive Illustration.

First impressions

● Read the words below from *The Worst Witch*. They describe how Miss Hardbroom speaks to, or looks at, Mildred.

nastily	icily	stony glare	bitterly
coldly	wearily	snapped	frosty glare

● How does Miss Hardbroom feel about Mildred?
● Which adverb suggests that she is exasperated by Mildred?
● Read the quotations below from the first four chapters. They describe Mildred's behaviour when Miss Hardbroom is cross with her.

Mildred hastily blew out the candle and dived under the bedclothes.
Mildred blushed. 'I'm sorry, Miss Hardbroom,' she muttered.
'I … let it in, Miss Hardbroom,' Mildred said hesitantly.

● How does Mildred behave when Miss Hardbroom is displeased with her?
● Which word suggests that Miss Hardbroom makes Mildred feel unsure of herself?
● Do Mildred's and Miss Hardbroom's feelings towards one another change during the course of the book? Give reasons for your answer.

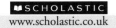

Talk about it

News team

● Use this page to plan your news report.

Newsreader(s): _____

Outside reporter(s)/interviewer(s): _____

Those to be interviewed:

_____ played by _____

_____ played by _____

_____ played by _____

Newsreader's opening introduction – setting the scene:
(Include key points: where, what, when, who.)

_____

_____

_____

Open questions: (Why? How? In what ways?)

Addressed to _____:

_____

Addressed to _____:

_____

Newsreader's summary, closing the news report:

_____

_____

Get writing

Antonyms and parody

> **Objective:** To explore how writers use language for comic and dramatic effects.
> **What you need:** Copies of *The Worst Witch*, photocopiable page 28, thesauruses.
> **Cross-curricular link:** Music.

What to do
● Re-read the school song from Chapter Two. List the nouns the author uses to sum up its content, such as *pride, joy* and *striving.* Ask: *Which verb is used rather than* singing *to demonstrate how the pupils perform the song?* (*Droning.*)
● Discuss why, if the song is full of *pride, joy and striving,* the young witches should drone rather than sing brightly.
● Suggest that, sometimes, when words conflict with experience, people will write a parody of a song, poem or story. They keep the basic construction, in recognisable form, but change some of the words.
● Hand out copies of photocopiable page 28. Ask the children to find the words in the original text and then list 'antonyms' or opposites. They may put more than one choice, as in the first example.
● Finally, invite the children to rewrite the school song as a parody that Mildred might sing in private to make herself laugh. Allow the use of thesauruses to find antonyms of matching syllables.

> **Differentiation**
> **For older/more confident learners:** Challenge the children to alter lines for added humour, such as Verse 2, Line 4 – *Spells and charms shoved up our vests.* Ask: *Can you make up a tune for the school song?*
> **For younger/less confident learners:** Provide a close-procedure copy of the song with appropriate gaps for children to write their new words. Display a tabletop alphabet to help the children navigate the thesaurus.

Descriptive names

> **Objective:** To group and classify words according to their meanings.
> **What you need:** Copies of *The Worst Witch*, photocopiable page 29.

What to do
● List the surnames of characters in *The Worst Witch.* Ask why the author chose these names. (For example, *Hubble* rhymes with *trouble* and might evoke the *bubble* of a cauldron.)
● Can the children think of a new surname for themselves if they were a witch or wizard? (*Miss Cobweb* or *Mr Wand.*)
● Look together at Chapter One where Maud and Mildred are discussing names for their kittens. Ask: *How did Maud explain her choice of 'Midnight'?* (*It sounds dramatic.*)
● Hand out copies of photocopiable page 29.
Go around the class asking each child in turn to complete the sentence *The witch's kitten is a… kitten* using an adjective with the next letter of the alphabet. (For 'x' allow an adjective such as *exciting.*) Ask the children to note the adjectives on their sheet.
● Invite the children to choose a few adjectives, and make up names (nouns) for the kittens, to reflect the meaning of the adjectives.

> **Differentiation**
> **For older/more confident learners:** Ask the children to write about themselves in the third person, using their adopted 'magical' name (such as Jack Sparkle), and explain how and why they chose the name they did for their kitten, adding a detailed description of the kitten.
> **For younger/less confident learners:** Write adjectives on cards for children to sort and copy alphabetically.

Get writing

Appearance and demeanour

> **Objective:** To use settings and characterisation to engage readers' interest.
> **What you need:** Copies of *The Worst Witch*, enlarged copy of Extract 1.

What to do
● Display Extract 1, and highlight the third paragraph, which describes Miss Hardbroom. Underline each adjective: *tall, terrifying, sharp, bony, black, tight, stretched*. Ring the word *scragged* and discuss its meaning and effect (it is stronger than *scraped* or *pulled*).
● Invite the children to find words that describe Miss Hardbroom's manner and style of moving (*door crashed open; swept out into the corridor*). Highlight adverbs that show how Miss Hardbroom spoke or looked (*nastily, icily*).
● Ask why there is a detailed description of Miss Hardbroom, but not of Miss Bat. (She is not a main character; has a passive role.) Remind the children that Miss Bat is the chanting mistress.
● Ask the children to try and envisage Miss Bat. They could ask themselves: *Is she taller or shorter than Miss Hardbroom? What are her hair and eyes like? How does she move and speak?*
● Challenge the children to write a description of Miss Bat as Form One arrive for a special chanting lesson.

> **Differentiation**
> **For older/more confident learners:** Ask pairs to swap their descriptions and question each other about Miss Bat's appearance or behaviour. Encourage them to re-read and refine their work.
> **For younger/less confident learners:** Discuss the meaning of 'chanting' and explore how the subject Miss Bat teaches might influence her mannerisms and movements. Together, list useful adjectives to describe her.

Learning a skill

> **Objective:** To write non-narrative texts using structures of different text types.
> **What you need:** Copies of *The Worst Witch*, whiteboard and pens, photocopiable page 30. (If available: teach-yourself style craft books; skipping ropes, bouncy balls, stopwatches, craft materials.)
> **Cross-curricular links:** Art and design, PE.

What to do
● Re-read the description of how to ride a broomstick in Chapter Two. Demonstrate how learning such a skill could be presented in other ways – for example, using numbered instructions and abridged text (*1. Order stick to hover, 2. Sit on stick, 3. Give it a sharp tap*).
● Show how a box or star could be used to present a tip.
● Scribing for the whole class, rewrite the section on the difficulties involved, using the first person. (For example: *It had taken Mildred took me several weeks of falling off and crashing before she I could ride reasonably well…*)
● Invent advice on persuading kittens to ride, using bullet points: *Keep kitten calm by stroking, Do not feed kitten immediately before riding*, and so on.
● Discuss the differences in presentation and style between the original narrative and the new text.
● Hand out copies of photocopiable page 30. Ask the children to choose a skill from the list or write about a skill they have or are learning and complete the activity.

> **Differentiation**
> **For older/more confident learners:** Challenge the children to make a short presentation to the class based on their completed sheet. They may use visual aids.
> **For younger/less confident learners:** Suggest that children work together in pairs to complete the photocopiable sheet.

Get writing

Rules and regulations

> **Objective:** To group related material into paragraphs.
> **What you need:** Copies of *The Worst Witch*, whiteboard and pens.
> **Cross-curricular link:** Art and design.

What to do
- When the children have read Chapter Nine, ask why Miss Cackle is afraid of turning the snails back into witches.
- Display paragraph five of rule number seven in the Witches' Code: *anyone having been changed into any type of animal … any form of magic against their captor.*
- Ensure the children understand the word *captor* and invite comparison with its converse, *captive*, and the verb *capture*.
- Discuss what the main part of *rule number seven* might be. (Witches must not use transformation magic against another witch.)
- Explain that subsections or paragraphs are used in legal documents. Show how rule number seven might be presented. (*Rule 7, subsection (i): except for purposes of self-defence; subsection (ii): if self-defence has been used, the captive is not permitted to practise magic upon their captor.*)
- Challenge the children to write their own Witches' (or Wizards') Code, making sure that each rule covers a different aspect of magic, such as wands or broomsticks.

> **Differentiation**
> **For older/more confident learners:** Challenge the children to create a list of assigned punishments for witches and wizards who break the code. (For example: confiscation of wands for a period of time; broomsticks being temporarily grounded.)
> **For younger/less confident learners:** Support children working in groups, and form the basic rules together, exploring how subsections work.

Half-day holiday

> **Objective:** To vary pace and develop viewpoint through the use of direct and reported speech, portrayal of action and selection of details.
> **What you need:** Copies of *The Worst Witch*, enlarged copy of Extract 3, writing materials.

What to do
- Display Extract 3 and read it together. Invite the children to look carefully at how the author shows what is happening through:
  - Description – such as Mildred's *blushing, stumbling, tripping*, Miss Cackle's *beaming*
  - Statement – such as other girls' behaviour (*The girls laughed.*)
  - Direct speech (*'You may sit down girls.'*)
  - Implication (*heroine* in inverted commas)
  - Action – *everyone stood up*; *twisted her fingers, flung an arm…*
- Re-read the closing line of the extract. Can the children guess/remember what happens next?
- Invite the children to discuss with a partner what might happen after Maud and Mildred run off at the end. Ask questions such as: *Will the afternoon go as planned? If someone spoils their afternoon, who is it likely to be; how and why?*
- Ask the children to plan and write a short story, titled *The Half-day Holiday*, in which Mildred and Maud are the central characters.
- Remind them to use different narrative techniques to retain the reader's interest and vary the pace of their story.

> **Differentiation**
> **For older/more confident learners:** Invite pairs of children to read aloud and evaluate each other's work.
> **For younger/less confident learners:** Offer tighter plot guidance such as: *Maud and Mildred meet some young wizards from a nearby Wizard's Academy. They show off and have a wands' fun-fight that goes wrong. How do they sort out the problem?*

Antonyms and parody

● Find antonyms or contrasts for the words and phrases and write them in the right-hand column. Some suggestions are given, but you may add more of your own.

● Use a thesaurus to help you.

Words	Antonyms
onward	backward, downward, zig-zag
proudly	
straight	
true	
never a day	weeks and weeks
kept	left
bubbling	
nicely	
joy	
working	
think of	

● Copy out the school song from Miss Cackle's Academy for Witches (in Chapter Two). At the same time, replace the listed words with your new words to create an amusing parody.

SECTION
6

Descriptive names

Initial	Adjective	Name
a		
b		
c		
d	dramatic	Midnight
e		
f		
g		
h		
i		
j		
k		
l		
m		
n		
o		
p		
q		
r		
s		
t		
u		
v		
w		
x		
y		
z		

My favourite kitten name is: _____

Learning a skill

My skill is _____

Materials I need are _____

How to start: _____

Practice (How? How often? How long?): _____

_____

Self-assessment and progress notes: _____

_____

Improvements: _____

_____

Setbacks: _____

_____

gymnastics	sew on button	trampoline	ice-skate
skateboard	dance	bake cake	ride pony	yo-yo
swim	knit	tie knot	weave	sew	juggle
ride bike	origami	play recorder	skip	judo

SCHOLASTIC
www.scholastic.co.uk

READ & RESPOND: Activities based on The Worst Witch

Assessment

Assessment advice

The Worst Witch offers a number of areas for assessment. Observe if the children can recognise traditional aspects of British school-life in Miss Cackle's Academy: gymslips, satchels, writing lines, school songs, wooden benches. Can they identify such aspects as being distinct from those that are uniquely 'magic', such as cauldrons and potions? Ask them to relate magic lessons and learning goals to what they know of real-life secondary school: chemistry classes, how laboratories differ from classrooms, what significant school exams exist, and which used to take place, such as O (Ordinary) levels at age 16 and A (Advanced) levels at age 18, replacing respectively the yet earlier Matriculation and Higher School Certificate. Open discussion to determine children's understanding of when 'bossiness' or 'teasing' become 'bullying'. Note their interpretations of how Mildred deals with

Ethel's actions and the outcome. Are the children able to apply what they learn from Mildred to situations, real or hypothetical, in their own school-life?

Listen to the children explain how and why Miss Hardbroom's behaviour and attitude is plausible and consistent. Ask why this is important in fiction. (So that readers can identify with situations.) Can they explain and justify the teacher's 'pleasant grin' when announcing the shortage of black kittens? Can they determine if, overall, she is a force for good or bad? Look for text-related explanations. Discussing whether her treatment of the girls is fair will help assess how far the children have understood the implications of, for example, the witches having a good-natured nickname for their teacher, and voiced recognition, towards the end, that she is not all bad.

Mixed feelings

> **Assessment focus:** To infer characters' feelings in fiction and consequences in logical explanations.
> **What you need:** Individual copies of *The Worst Witch*, photocopiable page 32, writing materials.

What to do
● Briefly discuss the ending of the book. Ask: *Was it a satisfying ending? Why? How has the author managed to create an ending that opens the opportunity for further stories, while ensuring this story stands alone and complete in its own right?* (Discuss how the relationship between Mildred and Maud and their teacher is developing and changing, with greater mutual respect; characters and setting strongly established inviting further adventures, this only being their first term.)
● Explain that most people in fiction, as in real

life, are neither all good, nor all bad. Hand out copies of photocopiable page 32 for the children to complete. Remind them that they may want to refer to the text of the book to qualify and explain their answers to some of the questions, and to support their expressed opinions.
● Point out that, if they do not have enough space to answer any particular question, they may carry on overleaf, marking each respective response with the number at the head of the question.
● Encourage the children to quote directly from the book if appropriate, reminding them to use quotation marks.
● Most of the questions relate to characters' feelings, interaction and behaviour. The fourth question, however, explores their understanding of the word structure and meaning of Hallowe'en.

Assessment

SECTION 7

Mixed feelings

● When you have finished reading *The Worst Witch*, answer these questions.

1. Circle the quotation below that relates to Mildred Hubble:

    "word perfect as always"   **"her spells always worked"**

    "several weeks of falling off and crashing"

2. Why do you think Mildred has lots of friends?

_____

3. Fill in the missing name:
   "Miss Hubble never made any icy remarks to her. Because of this,

   _____ was often rather bossy with the other girls."

4. Do you agree this person is bossy? Is she more than just bossy?
   Explain your answer with reference to the text.

_____

5. The apostrophe in the word Hallowe'en shows that one letter is missing.
   What is the missing letter? _____

6. Ring the word below that shares the meaning of e'en.

       eyes   **event**   **elves**   **evening**   **exam**

7. After Mildred overheard the wicked witches' plot, she could still have run
   away from school. Why did she decide to go back?

_____

8. Would you have done the same as Mildred? Explain why.

_____

_____

_____

SCHOLASTIC
www.scholastic.co.uk